ANCHOR BOOKS

A CELEBRATION OF VERSE

Edited by

Neil Day

First published in Great Britain in 2001 by
ANCHOR BOOKS
Remus House,
Coltsfoot Drive,
Peterborough, PE2 9JX
Telephone (01733) 898102

HB ISBN 1 85930 950 X
SB ISBN 1 85930 955 0

FOREWORD

This special anthology offers a unique collection of poetic expressions and inspirations on life and the world around us. Featuring accessible poems that can be enjoyed by all, we are sure that there is something here for everyone. Each poem is communicated across the barriers and helps develop that vital bond between reader and author.

Anyone who ventures within these pages will be treated to a host of delightful and engaging poems delivered in earnest from the poetic heart.

Read on and enjoy the unique gift of poetry at its best.

Neil Day
Editor

CONTENTS

WILL-O'-THE-WISP

I feel you on a summer's breeze,
I see you chasing autumn leaves
And as I bend to kiss your lips,
You vanish like a will-o'-the-wisp.
At night when I dream you're here with me,
I hold you close and we sway dreamily,
Your lips brush mine, I hold your hand,
I'm in a magical wonderland.
Night slips by and dawn is breaking,
I awake, my heart is aching,
You're gone from me, how shall I exist?
My own beloved will-o'-the-wisp.
It seems to keep you here with me,
I must keep dreaming constantly.

E Timmins

REBIRTH AGAIN AND AGAIN

Why joy to watch the curious kittens prance?
Or relish playful puppies as they brawl,
Or see new lambs cavorting on a knoll,
As colts and calves unsteadily take stance.
The newly-born, when even glanced askance
Evoke ambitious yearnings in us all,
An atavism just beyond recall,
Vicarious retrieval . . . one last chance!

Maybe that in this new life, unbeguiled,
The inner joy of simply being alive
Will never dim and blameless, undefiled,
Stay unbesmirched until those days arrive
Replete old age, still like an artless child
Redeems us all . . . through such might we survive?

Patrick Brady

MEMORIES

I close my eyes and bring to mind your face
A smile so warm and full of kindness too.
Lines etched over years, I long to embrace
I close them tighter and I think of you.

Your eyes light up and glint like shafts of steel,
When tempers fired they blacken like the night.
Then wet with tears each time that you reveal
Stored memories of what was wrong or right.

Your mouth with words soft spoken on your lips
Lifting my heart upwards high to the sky
Then hard crashing down like waves on a ship
How was I to know your lips would lie.

I close my eyes and think of our romance,
It died before it ever had a chance.

Kathleen Morris

INTO THE VOID

Tolling bells afar across the marsh
Where Desolation blind and wary strays -
With evening mist my tears are shared, so harsh
That grim companion of my living days,
Whose soul and mine to kinship do aspire
In mad delirium of torment torn -
Where swirl dark deathly dancers of Hell fire
Into their slime whose depths have seen no morn . . .
Securing bonds which no daylight unties,
Caressing sightless eyes with tenuous hands . . .
My soul imploring all this night denies:
My wrestling mind cries: 'Freedom!' from this land,
From tentacles of darkness release find
That I may whole remain amongst mankind.

Carolyn Smith

SONNET FOR BEETHOVEN

Until your mighty music first was heard,
Of power and grandeur beyond space and time,
Till your creative spirit first was stirred
To work of such intensity sublime;

Never was music heard like this before,
Never again would music be the same;
Paintings in sound from earth to heaven would soar;
Such chords and melodies your power proclaim.

Artist, creator bold, you stand alone.
So lives forever your life's work supreme,
Inspiring and inspired, poems in tone,
The music from your heart as from a dream.

Though silenced ears denied you every sound,
The inner ear gave hearing more profound.

Joy Jenkins

THE DAWNING OF LOVE

Where a man gives a lass a knowing look,
Assuringly giving her the glad eye,
Perhaps giving her a gold leafed book,
As a gift, as he gently goes by.

The book is about poems all about love,
He can't put thoughts into words,
He could do with help from the good Lord above,
Doesn't know about the bees and the birds!

She slowly looked up and gave him a smile,
She blushed, she was so painfully shy,
His efforts had certainly been worthwhile,
It didn't look like an early goodbye.

He was glad he had made this special endeavour
And he knew that this love would go on forever.

Edith Antrobus

THE SECOND CHANCE

The second chance too seldom ours to own,
To stem the angry words best left unsaid;
To stay their mean, unworthy thoughts instead
And banish that which later must atone.
Or yet to heal the wounds ourselves alone
Have wreaked upon the undeserving head;
Lain festered in the days which lay ahead,
The guilt for which our wayward hearts have shed.

'Tis not for nought the scriptures swift to scold
The ones in haste to pass the other side.
Such chances miss which in our lives unfold
To do most good, lest least reward abide.
To squander soul in search of earthly gold
The smaller gain, a greater goal denied.

Mary Ryan

MY VALENTINE

For years we've known each other well
Your heart in harmony with mine,
And in your arms I love to dwell
I know I've found my Valentine.

Sometimes I think 'What can I do
To make the more, our hearts entwine?
How else, to show my love is true?'
I pray you'll be my Valentine,

These thoughts of you are ever fond,
To be with you is so divine
My heart with yours I love to bond,
Please darling - stay my Valentine.

Though I repeat this - year on year
My love for you stays strong and clear.

R L Shipp

THERE IS A LOVE

There is a love that's beyond all known love,
A pause on the lips, a dream in the eye,
A stepping stone to the glories above,
A love that sits ever enthroned on high.
There is an understanding that's deeper
Than any black hole wandering in space,
A love that surrounds a waking sleeper
And shows in every line upon the face.
There is a sealing bond so much stronger
That its unbroken nylon threads are kissed
By the years that unwind and grow longer
Until forgotten and buried in time's mist.
The love given to a child by a mother
Is carried to the grave like no other.

Pat Isiorho

SONNET FOR HEALTH

Sparkling streams rippling over the still rocks,
With bubbling, fresh, clean waters safely filled.
No sign of scum or fouling waste that killed
The lurking pike, or gathered by stout locks
Of deep-cut canal, edged by stone which mocks
The soft brown earth soon to be deeply tilled
To yield the crops and fruit that man has willed
For nourishment, carried in sack and box,
Safe from harmful fertilisers. Surely
We can hope for no less than wholesome food,
Clean, smokeless air we can breathe in purely?
Is it too much to expect that we would
Be able to know our needs are truly
Filled and provided with nothing but good?

Megan Smith

TRUE FRIENDS

No greater gift have I received
is the friendship you've shown to me
I will reach out to retrieve
your friendship which will forever be

With open arms, I welcome both of you
for you have shown me many things
in this friendship you've helped me through
my trust in you I will bring

In my heart your voices I hear
which through it all have helped me see
I no longer need to fear
for through it all we are free

Friends like you have no cost
so I pray this will never be lost.

Anna Pullen

DEAR MUM

I rose from sleep needed to weep because
I could not see the one I loved through laws
Of life and death on which I had no power.
I asked my Lord could yet she live this hour
Whilst I the journey made of many miles
To share her prayer with her and see her smiles
Once more before our Saviour took her home -
Where saints and mothers dwell and even some
Less worthy ones who know that something's wrong.
The hour was given and I sped on my way
Panic stricken, until I knew the hour
Was not an earthly time but heaven's bright day
When certain souls gathered beneath the bower
Are given what wonders there awaited them.

Pamela Jenner

THE SOUL

The soul is free, yet caged within my bones,
A stack of drawers that tower deep within,
With stories that lay dormant and untold,
A file of memories, filling to the brim.

Through time a drawer may softly close or open,
Flourishes of moods that are dispensed,
Whispering to me what is unspoken,
What remains unseen my mind dost sense.

The rage within my soul like dragon's fire,
Then peace and solace, music gently strums,
A sense of feelings sharp as thorny briar,
Till rich elation seeps and slowly comes.

For when my ashes blow, like grains of sand,
My soul will live, within the Promised Land.

Denise Oldale

LIFE IN THE FAST LANE

In our dressing gowns and drinking cocoa
You may well envy the champagne lifestyle
Playing 'The Ballad of John and Yoko'
All three get tedious after a while

You tire of all the sex, drugs and booze
As Jimi Hendrix blasts out 'Voodoo Chile'
Would you be offended if I refuse?
The packets of crisps and the pint of mild

Retirement, one of life's last great adventures
So I don't want a repeat of the last time
When you had forgotten to bring your dentures
And to eat that pork pie you borrowed mine

I was so embarrassed with nowhere to turn
When I won the first prize for the best 'gurn'.

John Smurthwaite

THE GARDEN OF MILLENNIA

Symbol of great beauty for all to see
The Statue of Millennia stands alone
In a woodland enwalled by Cornish stone
Embraced by branches of a walnut tree,
Protected by sacred statues of three
The sphinx, the lion and the unicorn
Displaying its single mystical horn
Enduring symbols of infinity.

The Temple of Zeus spells eternity
A Greek lettered pond and waterfall
Is inspiring hope, faith and charity
Hark, now listen to the sacred bird's call
Within the Garden of Divinity
Where the beautiful goddess towers tall.

M MacDonald-Murray

STRAWBERRY VALLEY

I look back at those days, with nostalgic sighs,
As I get older, the time really flies,
So come my friend, come with me,
Back to where our memories be,

Let's climb above the splendour, of the streets we once knew,
Where most have gone, they've only left a few,
Let's search for the sights and the sounds, that are there in our minds,
Come my friend, let's see what we can find,

We'll go back to the friendliest people, you could ever meet,
In the old terraced houses, street after street,
With streets full of children, all playing their games
And such friendly neighbours, remember their names,

There was 'Hynam' and 'Eynon', 'Cleavey' and 'Keach',
Just some names, that lived in our street,
Remember then the old lower road,
With 'Jenkins', 'Haywood' and 'Price',
Who would stick together, through thick and thin,
They were oh so friendly and nice,

Yes my friend, we'll remember and behold,
The steam from those engines of old,
Where they pilfered the coal, from the wagons,
To keep warm and protect them, from cold,

Where women would linger, fags all alight
And old men wore 'dai-caps', from morning till night,
With shifting curtains and shadows just gone,
Searching for gossip, that they could pass on,

But emerging my friend, is a new lower road,
Let's hope it will shape, with the same friendly code,
Where people will pull together and rally,
The second time around, in our 'Strawberry Valley'.

Bill Gabb

FREE

The tree that sways in the wind,
Life is such a precious thing,
Look around at the things we've got
And not the things we have not.
The bird that flies by,
It does not regret its flight
And wishes it could swim!
The smell of the earth
And the beginning of each day,
Whether it be pauper or millionaire,
We can only breathe the same air
And only see the same things,
That in life are free.

Christine McGrath

A DOG CAME INTO MY LIFE

Never again we said in pain,
But our cries were in vain,
Our last dog departing sadly,
Left us feeling bereft badly.

Now into our lives you came,
More than willing for a game,
Tall and big you grew,
But docile, to give you your due.

Naughty at times, you dig,
Maybe this is because you're so big,
Yet love you do show,
And behind me you move in tow.

I'm so glad you came into our life,
Because we'd been through such strife,
Now you do make me smile,
Even though I've to run after you a mile.

So much love to us you give,
Now with us that you live,
When a little sad do I feel,
Then my heart you do steal.

Your snout do touch my hand,
With a tongue that feels like sand,
'Be happy,' you try to say,
Keep all your sorrows at bay.

Susan Shaw

FEELINGS

The spark has gone together with the twinkle in my eye,
Where did it go? When did it leave and most important, why?
Yesterday was rosy, aromas fresh and new,
Everything was hopeful, now it seems untrue.
I cannot understand it, or figure out the reason,
Dark and dreary, dismal, damp, a depressing season.
What an effort to get up, to dress and go downstairs,
Much easier to stay in bed and snooze away my cares.
Through the window I can see a glimmer of the sun,
Peeping over the horizon, a rainbow has begun.
Oh, so much clearer now, a shadow on the glass,
Is that a daisy I can see, standing on the grass.
There'll be a new tomorrow, of that there is no doubt,
My spark and twinkle they are back, my misery washed out.

E M Gough

MY LOVE

Her beauty is the softest summer glow,
her eyes like morning dew upon the rose.
Her hair the lightest cloud I'll ever know,
a stance and step my simple mind o'erthrows.

Her thought is clear, a limpid crystal stream,
soft satin are the words she's moved to speak.
She listens too with eyes that ever seem
so full of loving welcome for the meek.

A spirit like the clearest day in spring,
a soul that kindly never turns away
from pain or grief or poorest suffering
man; constant like the light of every day.

But most of all my love your heart is warm
and always there to hold me in the dawn.

Jack W Oliver

EMERGENCE

Fog penetrating into a mind,
Filled with fear and desolation:
Where is hope and consolation?
Where peace to find,
And shadows no longer bind:
No more this desecration:
No more a fascination,
Of an evil kind.

Fog lifting up its shroud,
Revealing calm within:
Thoughts crying out loud,
Peace and hope begin,
Filtering through on a cloud
Free from a world of sin.

Josie Rawson

In The Air

There is a whisper in the air
That stirs the soul and makes hearts sing.
There is upon each sunrise
A half felt sigh of sweet surprise.
Love can last a thousand years
Or break the heart with bitter tears.
We can move on, or reminisce
Of sweet young love, with youth's first kiss
Of how it was meant to be
A lifetime's love, of you and me.

Gladys Mary Gayler

THE SEASONS OF LIFE

The song of my youth was rare as an orchid
full with the wonders of life and new things
every new day was filled with adventure
yet short lived as the late snows of spring.

My manhood was full with hard work and passion
I never stopped to count the years going by
why did I never realise I was so boring
and others around me living a lie.

My autumn is filled with tears and emptiness
walking alone with the ghost of my past by my side
leaving the words, the pages turning and turning
the days and the years just chapters in time.

Tomorrow if the sun shines I will find a new life
new places, new people, perhaps foreign climes.

Leslie P Allen

ILLUSION

Alone and wakeful on a winter's night,
Whilst watching shadows creep across the floor,
I thought I heard your footsteps, swift and light,
Ascend the stairs to pause close by my door.
Although ten dreary years, on leaden feet,
Had plodded by since your so sudden death,
I half-believed you had returned, my sweet;
And starting up in bed with quickened breath
And pounding heart, I called your name, dear wife,
Hoping to see no pallid ghost, but you
Restored by some great miracle to life.
So fond a fancy, in my heart I knew
To be illusion; yet, with eager eyes,
I watched for you till dawn lit up the skies.

John Clark

GEORGE

I am called George
And I live in a hutch
I eat lettuce and carrots
Which I like very much

A brown and white coat
And a nose that is pink
A cool water bottle
When I need a drink

I have straw and hay
Which makes a nice bed
But when they don't feed me
I eat straw instead

The door opens downwards
I jump on the ground
I hide in the flower beds
Until I am found

Watch out for the fox
For he's sly and crafty
I run home to my hutch
So safe although draughty

I like Nathan and Callum
I see them each day
They talk to me sometimes
And I watch them play

Sometimes I get lonely
When I'm in my house
My friend is the hedgehog
With a beautiful spouse

The life of a rabbit
Can often be great
But I wouldn't be lonely
If I had a mate.

T Rutherford

MY LOVE

Shall I compare thee to a bright red rose,
Thou art more passionate and beautiful,
Thy passion and love like the sun, glows,
Thou movst elegantly, never dull,
Thy passion and love shall shine eternally,
Like your memory, shall never expire,
Thou art fragrant, everyone will agree,
Thou burn in my heart like a wild fire,
I could compare thee to a furry cat,
Thou art twice as cute and just as kind
And I could go on to say more than that,
Thou hath enough passion and a great mind,
As long as I can breath and I can see,
So long lives me and I give life to thee.

Tom Syron

ALWAYS ON MY MIND

I climb down from my swing on the branch of a tree
And cradle up dolly so ragged and split.
I then run and skip along skylark and buttercup lee
Down to the brook where we picnic and sit.

As Daddy picks me up and swirls me around and around
Mummy tries, but only half, to grab my shoeless feet.
Then all puffed out and laughing, we all lay on the ground.
In that meadow, in that summer, in that love so complete.

Later, as we watch the sun sink into the brook
We hear the call of the pheasant and the waterhen's 'peep'.
We all hold hands, the four of us and to the stars we look.
Then, when I find my special star, I awaken from my sleep.

It's only then I realise and then my heart takes fright.
Mummy and Daddy became that star, which will shine forever.
It was painful to have lost them once
But I lose them every night.
I thank the Lord for the star that shines
And that they died together.

B Summers

MYSTERY OF LOVE

Love can be a wonderful emotion
    or a feeling deep within,
Love can be exciting and cause your head to spin
    like the churning movement of the ocean,
Love can make you worry and have silly notion
    it can make you bad or make you commit sin,
Love is what you give and try your best to win
    and can make you true and show devotion.

Love can make you calm and show mad rage
    can make you sober or become a drinker,
Love isn't measured there's nothing to gauge
    it can make you kind or become a stinker,
Love isn't beauty nor has any age
    it can have you caught, hook, line and sinker.

Leslie Holgate

MAN'S BEST FRIEND

(Inspired by Ecclesiasticus:4, 12-19)

Wisdom is a window to the heavens
The yeast of thought the intellect leavens
A baker's dozen fully understood
The staff of life baked seven times as good

The cornerstone of truth to make complete
The heart's desiring so to be replete
No fool nor cynic would she e'er abide
She sees too well the mocker to deride

Upon pure hearts alone she plies her quest
And shares her banquet with an honoured guest
'Tis wise to seek her out before your end
Pray God will deign to make of her your friend

But first she'll test you through her winding ways
Before she deigns to bless you all your days.

Cherry

A Song That Has Been Sung

A new-born baby so helpless
Can never be born again
An apple once fallen from a tree
Can never be the same.

Yet a song that has once been sung
I can sing all over again.

A life that has once been lived
Can't be lived all over again.
Angry words once spoken
Can't be taken back again.

They are like water running under a bridge
Sounding angry with too much rain.
Yet a song that has once been sung
I can sing all over again.

Audrey E Ritzkowski

A DAME'S SONNET
(Dedicated to Miss Elizabeth Taylor)

Once I saw a starlet virgin to screen
Whose siren's voice demean made sweetness pant,
In vision's prettiness scene by scene,
A dark mare's twin, spell star'd in friendships cant,
Her hardship rides, bleak moors - black winter's bay
Whose course and bends run like a gallop's dream,
Winnowing smiles from sadness's rough way,
To make life's beauty live in black's redeem.
So faithful lassie loved for deeds good dares,
A champion thor'bred by woe's passage,
'Gainst adversity's brunt, foes and wild cares,
Which roll in actions reel, dreamscopes' corsage,
To bloom an actress thane, a Dane of dames,
A rubied diamond silent shrew of pains.

Barry Bradshaw

THE SPIRIT OF POETRY

If chance should lead my wand'ring steps to stray
To craggy ledge where wild waters leap,
Plunging to unseen depths 'neath sun-drenched spray
To form a rainbow cloud above the deep.
And there I sense a presence so sublime
With thoughts of poetry, music or such muse,
To find an exaltation of the mind,
And glimpse a thousand words that I may use.
But all too soon the vision fades; 'tis spent,
And I will toil well past the midnight hour
Trying to grasp the rhythm, rhyme and sense
Of magic dwelling in that awesome power,
Encompassing all realms of heav'n and earth,
And blessing all who find it with re-birth.

John Wilson Smith

SONNET TO MY DEAREST LOVE

Your voice - a zephyr on the cool night air
the merry laugh that brightens up your face
the warmth and knowing that, for me, you care
your movements always soft and full of grace

and when I hold you close within my arms
in all the world I am the one most blessed
my stressful times only your presence calms
I'm joyful after having been depressed.

My very soul soars like a bird on high
touching the clouds - flying on angels' wings
I love you now and will until I die
you are my life - the song that my heart sings.

The gates of heaven open for my dove
we'll enter heav'n together dearest love.

Florence Broomfield

CRUEL TO BE KIND

The frail old lady sits silently in her chair,
Staring at the wall, endlessly rubbing her hands.
Her daughter hovers awkwardly, brushing her mother's hair,
At this very moment, not knowing where she stands.

Can she continue to care for this lady, so sweet,
Who is so sadly, dependent on her for life.
The demands are difficult and so hard to meet,
So much to consider, she herself a mother and wife.

Her mother knows nothing, her mind not her own,
She doesn't remember her present day thought.
Needs feeding and bathing, can't be left alone,
Doesn't know where she is, her memory so short.

Tearful and sad, she has made up her mind,
After all, the nursing home staff are sure to be kind.

F Mitchell

TOO MANY WHISPERS!

Tainted whispers from a meaningful song,
Fatal whispers corrupting an attraction,
Silent whispers are long past gone,
Strange whispers oddly causing a reaction.

Hot whispers trigger a sensual burning,
Cold whispers send your blood to chill,
Hurtful whispers explode a deep yearning,
Loud whispers make the world stand still.

Bad whispers you bury or put them aside,
Sweet whispers are imprinted in the mind,
Confused whispers so difficult to decide,
Cruel whispers are so terribly unkind.

Rich whispers so expensively sold,
Secret whispers still waiting to be told.

Michelle Duffy

OUR LIFE

I loved you from the moment our eyes met,
I couldn't fail to notice their deep blue.
You held me in your arms, I hoped and yet
Could not envisage life for just we two.

But when uncertain of our future life
I confided to you my greatest fears
You reassured me I would be your wife
And we would live together through the years.

The marriage vows we took ensured that we
Would always be together come what may
And when I think about our life I see
We kept the promises we made that day.

Of course a day will come when we will part
Then one of us will have a broken heart.

Catherine Craft

GLOBAL WARNING

O world, of love and beauty!
Nature's glory all around;
Sad, a devil's cruelty
in Man's own story found

O world, such creatures in it
of every shape and colour!
Man, selling off the planet
for an easy dollar

O world, an Eden bound to lose!
History, repeating our mistakes;
Lion kings born in eco-zoos;
Mercenaries, raising the stakes

O world, defying an ozone crack;
Beware! Nature's fighting back

R N Taber

SAVE THE CHILDREN

A new child is born, shall we weep or cheer
Or is this yet another mouth to feed
Just look around you, all is barren here
The earth unyielding will not quench their need

Our brothers are not able to survive
They search for food, but find that all is gone
Our sisters they have only love to give
No other way to help the little one

The flies torment and swarm their naked skin
The malnutrition makes their tummies swell
Their dark eyes show no lustre from within
What kind of place on earth is this to dwell

A new day has dawned, shall we laugh or cry
Or should we ask the daunting question - why?

Jean Birch

IN THE PARK

The park in winter. Leafless boughs hang bare.
In the sharp wind, a barking dog runs free.
White clouds sit coldly on the frosted tree.
A yawning desolation fills the air.
A solitary woman on a chair,
Unwraps a sandwich, chews it joylessly,
Pours out weak tea and drinks mechanically,
First streaks of ageing silvering her hair.

She shuts her eyes and pictures days gone by,
Her playful children chasing ball and dog.
Another life. Another age. Blue sky
Hung in the heavens then, not this grey fog
That smudges landscapes, blears the weary eye,
Squats in her heart as heavy as a log.

Sheena Blackhall

THE JOYS OF A SEASON

Sweet fragrances of summer linger in the air,
the world is full of colours to inspire the artist brush.
People seek the sunlight on beaches everywhere,
relaxing from life's toils there is no need to rush.

The summer makes the masses feel lazy,
children enjoy a long holiday from the routine of school.
The outlook for the future is bright and hazy,
or at least this is the general rule.

The most perfect of all the seasons,
created by God with man in mind.
For happiness there is so many reasons,
when nature is being so very kind.

Enjoy the summer while you can for winter approaches fast,
such pleasant times make the memories that will always last.

M A Challis

HERE'S TO OUR WORLD

'Here's to our world'
The beauty of all beauties
An island in space
The home of all our countries.
May her people's love surround her
With dignity and grace
With all the stars around her
As she spins along in space.

'Here's to our world'
So precious and so lovely
All through the years
The sun - her royal trophy.
May her reign be long and wonderful
As she journeys on her way
Her destiny - the Universe
As she rides the Milky Way.

And with her moon beside her
She fills our hearts with pride
Raise your glasses and salute her
Sing her praises far and wide
For she's our life - our world!
Our world!

Nelson Peters

THE SUNDIAL

The old grey sundial of weathered stone
Is just perfect in a way of its own.
The writing on it concludes with the rhyme
'Stay a while where sunshine and shade mark time'.

Eager young and old folk reach out to touch,
Over years it has reflected so much.
Steadfast it stands always tranquil and true,
Where we see sunshine and shade rendezvous.

The sundial speaks of eternal life,
Of adaptation to upsets and strife;
Blended rough and smooth, caressed by the sun,
It is telling the time as the hours run.

This sundial, surrounded by flowers
Bestows radiance on the passing hours.

Doris E Payne

AN ANGEL FOR BUFFY

There will come a time when we all must fight
Our inner demons that control the mind,
'Cos underneath it we're one of a kind
Blinded by the truth that is out of sight.
This is the journey we take in our plight
To save the humanity of mankind.
The love of you will always come to mind
To save the day like the sun after night
That makes every vampire run and hide
From all they fear like never before,
Because everyone has a darker side
That lurks underneath their flesh to their core.
But we all must believe and stand with pride
'Cos an Angel watches from heaven's door.

Amanda Jayne Biro

TAKING THE PLUNGE

Do I take the plunge or just stay right here?
Should I test the waters, what if they're too deep?
Will my mind just focus on unseen fear
Much too afraid to allow me to leap?

I stand and take just one more quick look
Hoping that my dread will subside in time
But, alas, the sneaky glance I just took
Has me running scared from my first big crime.

Could I dare? Would I ever be that bold
To grab on with both my outstretched hands,
To grip it firmly and to take a hold
Before it disappears from where it stands?

I'm going to jump, it's started to call,
Hello to love I'm now ready to fall.

Melanie L Brown

LOVE WAS BEFORE WORDS WERE: II

Until words descended we didn't know
Either the right or wrong, the good or bad,
We gesticulated and made dumb show;
It was a struggle, cold and meagre clad.
When making love we had no need of words
Returning as we do to that dark gyre
From whence we came where conscience was first stirred;
Amid the dark our knowledge grew with fire -
Let us forget all words we ever spoke
And meet again before new word is born.
No words were ever needed love to cloak
If I could meet you in that primal dawn
We'd float an ark above the earthly soak,
And sure but something good from that must spawn!

Martin Green

CHILDHOOD GIFTS

How can a clown always be so happy?
The painted face beams out, our worries, none,
He gives us a gift that lasts, never gone,
Older now, I remember that chappie,
His tears not real, his pants wide and flappy,
From the high wire to net he flew as a swan,
To make us laugh louder, a joke, he's one,
So long ago, still I wore a nappy.

My wrinkles still crease, thinking of his flaws,
The balloon would pop spraying out water,
Fun given to us his only main cause,
To crowd he was led, his pain, his slaughter,
He bowed once, twice and took all our applause,
Was he really happy? I ask. Daughter . . . ?

Caren Taylor

COME FOR ME

Don't leave me too long in my loneliness.
Don't desert me for longer than you feel you must.
Don't leave me despairing, my world in a mess.
Come for me soon, I know in you I can trust.

I know you won't leave me, depressed on my own.
I know you love me, you'll come to my aid.
I know that you hate it, to leave me alone,
For you told me you'd come, this promise you made.

Leave what you're doing for I'm pining away,
Forgo all the other things, put me first on your list.
Remember how I'm special, and come now, today,
Recall all our promises from our very first kiss.
Come for me. Come for me. Else I shall die.
Say you are coming or was your promise a lie?

Kathleen M Andrews

THE CHASE

O lantern brightly shine, but cast no light
Show me the way, but not those at my heel
This weary wind does snatch and fingers bite
And brings me closer to the touch of steel

My flesh is torn but not beyond repair
But woe is he, who caught it in the scruff
There is a one whose love and tender care
Will cancel out this night of rough's

So swiftly feet take flight but do not trip
Give me the strength to weaken sabre's chase
God hold me tight against this blood red drip
That threatens name and loyalty of face

And should they reach and make a void of me
Remember I was not their enemy

Catherine Campbell Rodgers

SPELLBOUND

Wonderful eyes of the very deepest blue,
Laughter lit, danced around those pools
Smouldering through lashes of changing hues
Tranquil gaze from those limped pools so cool.

Long lingering look of a lover's gaze
Melting the heart and into the soul bites
Caring nothing just walking in a haze
Suspended wings unseen, to highest heights.

Words unspoken, remain within the mind
Swimming beneath a maze of golden lights
Depth of feeling as of, no other kind
An abyss opens holding the gaze, so right.

Plunging into fathoms, do not lose sight
Souls meet, unite and dream into the night.

Sheila A Waterhouse

LOVE

Love makes us happy when we're feeling down.
The elderly need it as well as the young.
We wear a big smile instead of a frown;
Feeling contented the whole day long.
Love keeps us going when times get too tough.
Even bad weather will not bother us.
The sea looks quite calm, even though it's quite rough.
Love is quite splendid, that's what we've been told;
As people get married, upon falling in love.
Repeating their vows, like to have and to hold;
And pray to be happy to the Lord up above.
Love is for all kinds; the rich and the poor.
Love makes the world go round, that I feel sure.

Elaine Brookes

SONNET TO AN ARTIST

A garden of patchy grass and bushes overgrown
A broken-down shed, weeds and rotted things
His eyes saw nothing, just a picture already sewn
A canvas of imagined beauty had taken wings

His garden paintbrush transformed the dreary scene
A pond for wildlife and where water lilies grow
Bright yellow marsh buttercups in reed beds green
And a shady weeping willow bowing low

A corner with gazebo draped in clematis
A place to sit, behold the fragrant flowers
Bright shrubs and bushes touched by sunset's kiss
To delight and find contentment in the passing hours

An artist's gift, a moment's meditation
Turned blank canvas to a font of inspiration

Iris Owen

THE LAST TURNING

She walks alone, in long brown coat, no shawl;
Thin trails of smoke surmount the sober town.
All leaves are blown, stray snow is set to fall;
Each step is sure and every tree trunk known.
Her basket's lighter now, though not by much,
But one old man has jam and scones for tea.
The river's pale, a fairy's listless touch,
No boats, no skiff, no coiling swans to see.
Just one more bend, an ancient granite bridge,
And then the lights come on as dusk seeks night.
Same whitewashed cottage, gate, and ordered hedge -
But what will be her first, most-cherished sight?
Put down your bonnet, claim the rocking chair,
And dream of Lammas Fair, some lover there.

Brian Phillips

DESTINY'S CHILD

Deep-throated, his whisper caught in my ear
Death shared a cold, morbid secret with me
He held out a hand, bade me to step near
Frantic, I saw there was nowhere to flee

His smile raised hairs at the nape of my neck
And fear cursed my mouth with a sudden drought
To dust, all my bravery but a speck
Where dreams of triumph would all come to nought

My heart filled the air with its loud tattoo
And I struggled in nausea's warm embrace
Nothing could save me from this fate, I knew
This was the wrong time, in quite the wrong place

But death was insistent, refused to wait
And I, unable to run from my fate

Kim Montia

HAM-LETTERS
(With apologies to William Shakespeare)

2B or not 2B? That is the pencil:-
Whether 'tis clearer on the pad to scribble
The notes and missives of poor lexicology,
Or to print in decipherable form,
Using the pencil lead. Today, a pencil,
No more; and for a change try pen and ink
To convey words of love or mere business
In legible form. Communication -
A necessary link to keep us sane.
For no one is an island, that's the truth
As we depend on others in this world
If civilisation's to be maintained.
Illegibility no more exists
When fax and e-mails oust handwriting tools.

John W Skepper

LOVE

They met at the crossroads, for all to see:
They didn't hide from the public eye
The blanket of darkness came over the Lea
They had their love, they were not shy.

They walked, they talked and held hands:
No one else existed in his or her thoughts
Only in each other, there was no sound
However would the spell be broken if they were caught.

For all these years it had been this way,
How much longer could all this last?
Who could honestly say,
When all this would become the past?

Now in their old age, good times had gone:
They were married you see,
They still had each other, but for how long?
Until the end of Forever, whenever that may be.

They had fond memories of being together:
Could this not just go on forever?

Jill K Gilbert

WATER

Rapid beautiful fluid flows.
To engulf us we'd perish, yet to be short we'd perish.
Watching its up-flow, it grows.
In far off lands, it's something cherished.

Holding the silver cup, I turn the knob.
Bursting out it crushes, floods.
Human devastation, far-off sobs.
But to me it's just a watering fountain, sprinkling underneath shrubs.

As I turn to stand, I look up to the sky.
Clouds grow grey, and it starts to rain.
It falls down, people turn grey and sigh.
It always rains in England, but it can't be humanly claimed.

Because the rain is free,
And will forever more, do as it please.

Charlotte Western-Reed

HARVEST TIME PICNIC

Amber blotched wheat fields with ripe harvest swaying
gently in harmony, waits for harvest time folk
to spread freshly starched linen, with soft fraying
edges, over cream coloured daisies, tinted egg yolk

Ragged clothed children play in tattered straw hats
that catch the breeze, rustling their fathers' crops
who bent their backs tending carefully, lest rats
should discover and steal, their prized wheaten tops

Rain clouds gather mutely in wine coloured stains
that spatter down softly, on plump buxom wives
running, laughing for cover, glad of the rains
that nurtures the crop, that moulds their lives

Harvest time folk reap plump wheat, nature's gown
of amber smudged crop, jewel in their crown

Patricia Berwick

PLEASURE

I was walking by the riverside
When I saw you there.
You were playing with the children
They did not have a care.

They came running towards you
Laughing loud and clear,
You held your arms out to them
To hold them oh so dear.

When I turned to walk away
It hurt so very bad.
It was the things I wanted most,
The things I never had.

Maybe some day I will find someone like you,
Then my hopes and dreams might just come true.

E Riggott

ONCE UPON A SILENT NIGHT

It fell upon a silent night, on one Christmas Eve,
  As we watched the fir tree branches, sway gently in the breeze
And tiny flakes of purest snow fell gently upon our heads,
  And the branches from the Christmas tree, all were thinly coated.

The old men stood with their lanterns and sung in deep voice,
  A time for us to remember, a time for us to rejoice.
It takes me back to my childhood days, back to long ago,
  Remembering when we played snowball fights and rolled amongst
                                                    the snow.

Children breathed on their tiny hands to keep their fingers warm
  And with their innocent voices, a ring of angels they formed.
Noses red and cheeks aglow, as the light shone on their smiles,
  The Christmas carols that were sung could be heard from across
                                                    the mile.

Now old, we relax by our open fire, comfortable in our own home
                                                    we sit,
  Together up close, hand in hand, our own Christmas tree lit
And in a nearby church, we could hear the evening mass
  And the blessed children in their beds,
  Could hear the bells of a far off Father Christmas.

L E Richmond

WILLIAM IN KENSINGTON

It's a Saturday morning fit for kings,
To pick out their boxer shorts and small things,
At a later date . . . to be monogrammed,
In the department, He is corder-cammed.

From limousine, keeping a hush-calm,
He greets the store assistant, calls her 'Ma'am',
His crowning glory, cut in a quiet room,
Next, some trainers, vests, PE kit, a comb.

Crowds soon materialise on the shopping floor,
He is slow-coached, with bags towards the door,
Outside, throngs bow to a store TV screen -
Watching football, he is leaving - unseen.

Lorna Liffen

TO A DEPARTED FRIEND

O' love thou hast deserted me,
My trust in you has gone;
I live my life in solitude,
My loneliness is long.

Desertion sadness fill my world,
Where you no longer are;
My love sweet one
Where have you gone?
Your voice I cannot hear.

My heart lies broken
Upon this tainted turf;
But always there is hope
When I look upon the Earth;

The spring will surely come again;
The buds of May appear;
But sweet one I shall always miss
Your loving presence here.
The days are long,
The nights are cold,
Your loving arms;
I cannot hold.

O' joy of lovers' sweet embrace,
If only once more in my life
I could see,
Your smiling face.

Annie Overy

RELAXING IN THE COUNTRY

How I can watch
The clouds sail by,
Making out each shape
By the hour,
How I can feel the heat
from the sun,
Laying here is oh such
Fun.

The smell of the green grass,
And the birds fly pass,
Away from the outcry of the
City,
Why more people cannot join me,
It's a pity.

Instead of the horns, the sound
of the cows,
How I can feel the soft breeze
Against my skin,
Against the city life, the
Country wins.

A Bhambra

MOVING WINDOW

I am old, but I feel young, as I sit.
My world is my window, for all to see.
People pass me by, some look, or wait a bit,
Children just pull faces, or stare at me.

Everyone is bustling, as I sit still,
No one seems to notice that I'm here.
Rain or shine, I always seem to find the will
To smile, and wave a hand, to who is near.

My moving window is my life, didn't you know?
I sit here, quietly watching every day.
No one calls, chats to me, I miss this so,
Days go by, I age some more, along the way.

Will you miss me, moving window, when I'm gone?
An empty chair, is all that's left, to sit upon.

Michelle E Pickess

REALISATION

As I ran for the bus, so shiny and red
I tripped on the pavement and knocked my head.
As I looked up I began to see stars
I imagined that I was living on Mars.
A crowd gathered round, a policeman too,
Oh no! I thought I'm at the zoo.
I got to my feet as the crowd disappeared,
My head still ached and in the street lights
I saw what I feared,
I had laddered my tights.

Sue Wooldridge

OVERTURE

Sweet, long awaited baby, born today,
What awe inspiring presence do you bring
Into our world? Where for a while you stay,
To influence all with whom you dance and sing.

What thoughts and knowledge lie behind that look?
What peace and love have you left far behind?
Have you a mission written in God's book?
Will we entwine together in one mind?

May love be with us in our family.
God give us all His strength to care for you,
To nurture, and to set your spirit free,
To fulfil all that you have come to do.

So darling grandchild from my heart I say,
'Welcome into this world, where you must play.'

Doreen Lawrence

ODE TO THE SUMMER SUN

She rises each morning, in gradual light,
With a golden smile, through the mists and haze,
Such warmth she brings, such happy days,
In the midst of summer, she shines so bright,
Like a burning fire, in the summer's height,
We depend on her in so many ways,
We lie in worship, an excuse to laze,
In her daylight hours, she reigns with might.

Trees with their blossoms, reach out tall and proud,
Bright flowers salute her, perfume sweet,
Snowdrops and daffodils, modest in the crowd,
Delicate roses, fragrant jasmine, a treat,
When the sky is overcast, there's a silver lined cloud,
And we feel at one with nature, such a magical feat.

B M Foster

FASHIONABLE MORALITY

Morals are no longer Bible encased.
Christians have become an outdated few
as they worship, singly, in their family pew
with fashionable ethics computer based.

Employment's basic aim is making cash
- machines have superseded human skill -
so, even parent partners, earn still
while offspring, foster cared, bring no backlash.

Variety in sex, they claim, for a full life
as well as bouncing play and pleasure,
sun, beach, sports field, ice-slope leisure
and night-long dancing where soft drugs are rife.

Still, Christian couples, sharing joy and tears
remain faithful and in love, for years and years.

Andrew Kerr

SUMMER

Smell seaweed fresh
Hot sand tickling toes
Awakens summertime

Corn standing tall
Sunshine's burning hot
Scythe swishes long.

Kathy Hill

TANKA

Is there any blight
on the reticulate rose
that the full moon throws
on to my door and window?
Can there be any perfume?

Jeffrey A Pickford

HAIKU POETRY

Wind wails summer lost
Leaves float effortlessly down
Clocks go back.

Dappled mellow sun
Mahogany brown conkers
Reflect the rain.

Watered silver webs
Hunting spiders lurk
In gossamered silk.

Charcoal-leaden skies
Rain hammers on wet windows
Blackbird hides in conifers.

Holidays fades fast
Summer has burnt itself out
Filled with fiery sun.

Northerly west wind
Brown leaves accumulating
Cat shivers in porch.

Spring stirring dead soil
Yellow crocuses budding
With pale primroses.

Judy Studd

ADORATION

'I love you so much,'
He said, gazing in the mirror
Which hung before him.
'We must never part,'
But the glass cracked lengthwise,
Conceited face distorted.

Ann Harrison

TRANSCONTINENTAL HAIKU

Africa, my birth place
cradle of humanity
denied or not

From Oslo to Rome
the European puzzle
slowly unravels

Millions still believe
in the American dream
mistaking trash for gems

In the Outback
I dreamt of snow storms
capping Ayers Rock

The Chinese claim
Hangzhou to be paradise
a bridge to heaven

The Falkland Islands
Malvinas to the Argentines
and always the birds

Bangladesh flooded
all the tears of the world
since Adam and Eve

Albert Russo

PRECIOUS MOMENTS

A warm summer day,
water shimmering in the
gold rays of the sun.

Dragonflies flitting,
delicate transparent wings
reflecting the glow.

The buzzing of bees
covered in pollen, as they
seek out each flower.

The rustle of leaves
as a gentle breeze begins
to blow through the trees.

Lying in the field,
the warm, soft grass beneath me,
enjoying the peace.

Keeping my eyes closed,
I listen to the birds sing,
soaring in the sky.

Time seems to stand still.
Distant sounds distract my thoughts,
breaking the moment.

Peace, like pleasant dreams,
is gone for now. Memories
will surely linger.

A Odger

MOUNTAIN

Climb up the mountain,
absorb the world around it.
Come back to the Earth,
keep the sights inside your mind.
Revisit, in times of need.

Andy Monnacle

TRUTH

Underneath image,
lies the element of truth.
Waiting to be found,
before it expires forever.
Buried, uselessly, unused.

Danny Coleman

LIFE

Live life to the full,
take no prisoners, be free.
When death approaches,
smile, with a satisfied smile.
Ensure there is life to take.

Mandy Ann Cole

PURE MAGIC

Springtime's door now stands ajar
Russet colours decaying, as winter's fade
Mother Nature's patchwork suddenly ablaze
Welcoming season's warmest spring star
Woodlands swaying pink floral's gold bar
Sleepy meadows creating potters glaze
Spring's awakening from her foggy deep haze
Gloomy winter days seem distant and far
Rainbows capture nature's pastel painted kite
Flattering crystal skies, embrace blossoms bow
Carpeting hillsides, where dancing heathers unite
Delicate baby seedlings, gentle start to grow
Whispering warm breezes, sweet cloudless delight
Sweet Mother Nature's spring rivers flow.

Ann Hathaway

SOLSTICE

A swivelling eye
beneath the sand blinks slowly.
The ocean shivers.

On gorse-clad hillsides
linnets' crimson turns to brown:
winter approaches.

A feathery snowflake
stirs the sun-kissed precipice.
The mountain quivers.

The glittering moon
sinks behind sinister clouds.
Darkness encroaches.

Blinded by headlights,
a lord of life lies mangled
in a stink of fox.

A bloodstained robin,
run through by a rapier,
seeks a cold nesting.

Rooted in thin scree,
the blood-red rowan bends down
to friable rocks.

Last summer's cygnet,
neck bowed back beneath its wing,
is surely resting.

Awaiting windfalls
vultures foregather, hunchbacked,
at the village end.

Dawn. A feeble sun,
a visitant from Hades,
begins to ascend.

Norman Bissett

THANKS TO MONEY

Life in luxury
Ends meeting in harmony
Credit: Midas touch

Rags are now riches
Nobody, a somebody
All thanks to money

Coined out of gold coins
Noted, some are counterfeit
Sometimes not genuine

A bleak heritage
Luck and buck wearing the day
Reaping a harvest

The sun shines daily
And gives away to the night
The dark awaits light

Genie and genius
Can turn many lives around
Canaan; are they bound

From the seed, it grew
Money-making myriad's brew
A new legal tender

It rose, now evil
Cast in different levels
Mankind now ditto

Grace greeted grass
But it was never the mass
For better or worse

Richer or poorer
Judgement would call on these three
Money, good, evil

Ato Ulzen-Appiah

THE COLD WINTER'S SURRENDER

The woes and the wails
Of the cold winter gales
How now they are subsiding
On flighted wing
The birds come to sing
A new spring is so exciting

While summer still sleeps
The white snowdrop peeps
Like a bride in virginal splendour
The sun o'er the meadows
Comes chasing the shadows
At last the cold winter's surrender

John Geehan

BEREAVEMENT

When tears cloud our eyes
In time of deepest sorrow
Our grief seems endless
Sorrow is but memory
Of a happy yesterday
Memory lives on
As all sorrow fades away
Leaving a new strength and peace

Val George

HAIKUS

The breeze blew gently.
The leaves wafted in the air.
They whispered softly.

They changed their colours
From green to mahogany
And russet and red.

Dropping leaves rustled.
They covered the waiting ground:
A Persian carpet.

Joyce M Turner

OUR TREE

The tree in autumn
Dressed to hold the golden light
Reflects the sunsets.

The tree in winter,
Death, beautiful in piled snow,
Just gently sleeping.

The tree in springtime
Revived and bursting with life
Holds promise unknown.

The tree in summer
Glory to behold, and now
The promise fulfilled.

Ruth Moser

SUM

Life's made of tiers;
the accumulating years
adding to the sum:
till life's final subtraction
prove the equation done.

I M Brown

FIVE HAIKUS

A pulled cork signals
a neck to mouth harmony
and thirst's fulfilment.

Clouds, old statesmen who
lie on the rich blue baize of
heaven and debate.

Sleep moors the tired
bodies of wearied souls in
a bed's soft haven.

Winter jasmine climbs
to entwine high trellis with
day's pale lemon stars.

The poetry book
open upon the table
invites the reader.

Dennis Marshall

ICICLES

Cold, hard and brittle
Like diamonds they hang
The thaw always comes

Barbara Tunstall

THE TANKA

Life is lifeless
each realise
as each dies
birth is speaking
death is silence

Ghazanfer Eqbal

BUTTERFLY

trapped butterfly:
wings beating against the pane
at the top - freedom

Geraldine Laker

AT ABOUT FOUR-THIRTY

snow
piled high
at
the
door

and waited

it
would have
been
cruel to
let
it in
you said

Brian Parvin

WHAT NOW!

Sing a song of sixpence a pocket full of rye,
Sing a song of sixpence, my momma why d' you die?
Sing a song of sixpence; the time has gone so fast,
Sing a song of sixpence, you're now part of my past.

Where do we go from here, where does it take me to?
I am the mother; I've taken the place of you.
Where will it lead me to, what do I have to be?
Now I've become you, my children must be me.

Sally Boyle

TRUST

Keep your eye simple
Your mind free of greed
Open yourself
To receive all you need
Look at the birds
See how they feed
They trust in nature
Give thanks with
Their songs
The universe knows
We all belong
Where are our songs
Where is our trust
Accept the universe
Is abundant with love
It takes care of its own
When we open our hearts
And we start to trust.

J Smyth

IMPRESSIONS OF ENGLAND

April storm behind me
Sun gleaming on a drake's head
Standing in jonquils.

Late summer evening
Walking in a sunken lane
Bats swoop overhead.

Ginger cat playing
In branches of yellow tree
On damp spring morning.

Christine Pleasants

AUTUMN

Autumn is fast approaching
Balmy summer days now gone
Leaves and petals falling
Birds no more in song

Colder crisper days ahead
Thoughts of summer fading
We wrap up warm
Against the wind
Which is all embracing

Nature has excelled herself
With colours to grace a canvas
Hues of red, brown, orange and yellow
Vibrant, yet mellow

It's a tapestry of colour
Its beauty awe inspiring
To capture these colours
With the stroke of a brush
Is an artist's dream

With colours ever changing
From yellow ochre to russet
Likened to an artist's palette
It's nature's way
Of playing tricks with us

Animals think of hibernation
Gardens take on a sparse look
In a moment sublime
Captured in time
The last petal falls

Phyllis Lorraine Stark

SUMMER

A kingfisher seen streaking by
A flash of blue past the eye
Mist drifts from the dew
Summer sun begins to rise on cue
Mornings by the river, a fascinating view.

A pair of dragonfly rapture
Jointly responding to the call of nature
Bulrushes sway in warm breeze
Beams of sunlight between leaves of trees
Listening to the wings of busy bees.

Trout breaks water surface nearby
As it splashes to take a fly
A heron standing very still
While waiting patiently to make a kill
A moorhen gives out a characteristic shrill.

A water-vole scurries to burrow
Its breeding partner quickly decides to follow
Mallards making a secret nest
Hiding it carefully in rushes to invest
Wildlife is sure to maintain the interest.

Brian Bates

ONE YEAR OF YOU

With autumn's chill breath
the tree casts off its children
and grieves grey and shapeless

Summer the lover
ecstasy when in her arms
sadness as she cools

Winter so unloved
welcomes the little robin
that brightens her gloom

Thirsting to drink the
sea when one glass of water
brings satisfaction

Joyous spring as frogs
turn the water into an
untuned piano

The moon, pleasing all,
shines as bright in the garden
as on the nation

Wilson John Haire

HIDDEN HEART

Hearts break instantly
with a look, a word, a touch
not to beat as strong.

Nor to give again
themselves recklessly to love
but hide from passion.

Karen Baynton

SAYING GOODBYE

Your face betrays you,
Your bright smile belies your pain.
Your pride excludes me.

Joan M Smith

EARTH

No one sees the bleeding
Tears are falling
Fire is burning
Something's twisting
Darkness is brooding
Our mother is yielding.

David Sparkes

LIFE GOES ON!

When you're feeling under par
Contemplate and prepare,
Search for every rainbow and wish upon a star!

Does it really matter who or what we are?
We are programmed to repair
When you're feeling under par!

Whether we eat fish and chips or caviar,
Live a simple life or one with flare,
Search for every rainbow and wish upon a star.

Energetic trekking or travelling by car,
Changing lifestyles takes us unaware,
When you're feeling under par.

Fish in tanks or tadpoles in a jar
Demand survival as we stop and stare,
Search for every rainbow and wish upon a star.

Life's promises can be near or far
To cherish and to share.
When you're feeling under par
Search for every rainbow and wish upon a star!

Denny Rhymer

THE LARKS FLY HIGH

Such beauty all around us lies
We humans need to look and stare
The larks fly high and fill the skies.

Their shape and deftness there belies
To emulate we would not dare
Such beauty all around us lies.

For us there is no compromise
Oh how we wish that we could share
The larks fly high and fill the skies.

We just look up and see the prize
Their love of freedom unaware
Such beauty all around us lies.

God looks down and on us relies
And men can never say they care
The larks fly high and fill the skies.

To help them when we hear their cries
Till love for creatures is not rare
Such beauty all around us lies
The larks fly high and fill the skies.

Margaret Williams-Dougliss

SHOW YOUR LOVE

Are the words you utter true
When you say that you love me?
The truth is there in what we do.

Words are like the rainbow's hue
That quickly fades, so prove to me -
Are the words you utter true?

My heart's afraid of losing you.
My love, my life wrapped up in thee.
The truth is there in what we do.

Show your love for me in all you do
As I try to show you constantly.
Are the words you utter true?

Let both of us begin anew,
My love for you - your love for me.
The truth is there in what we do.

And a stronger love will see us through
Our future years in harmony.
Are the words we utter true?
The truth is there in what we do.

V Finlay

THE EVER PRESENT SPIRIT

You left but we are not alone,
Your presence is here with us always;
We trust as your word has shown.

Your seeds of love were early sown,
We remember with joy nowadays;
You left but we are not alone.

We praise you and do not moan,
Faith in you brings forth our praise;
We trust as your word has shown.

We know your spirit as we roam
We scan the heavens with our gaze;
You left but we are not alone.

When in pain we so often groan,
Life sometimes seems like a maze;
We trust as your word has shown.

You promised us an eternal home,
Your holy spirit makes our spirit blaze;
You left but we are not alone.
We trust as your word has shown.

Joy A Davies

SMALL HAPPENINGS ARE EACH DAY'S SPAN

Now that I have grown so old
I live my life in a small span.
Small happenings do my life enfold.

Activities are not so bold
Now I do just what I can.
Now that I have grown so old.

In my mind my past is told.
Now once I roved, and once I ran.
Small happenings do my life enfold.

Esme, my dog, with me grows old;
(Though she to leap and run still can.)
Now that I have grown so old.

Prayer, music, reading, each day's gold,
With something from the TV can
Small happenings do my life enfold.

Lunch each week with friends as old
Happiness in such a little span.
Now that I have grown so old;
Small happenings do my life enfold.

Frances Joan Tucker

WHERE, OH WHERE?

Oh, my love, where can you be?
I yearn to clasp you close again;
So long I've searched in vain for thee!

Why hidest thou, thyself, from me,
Not revealing where nor when?
Oh, my love, where can you be?

I fly from place to place to see
If you bask by beck or ben:
So long I've searched in vain for thee!

I strain my eyes o'er hill and lea;
Across the fields of labouring men;
Oh, my love, where can you be?

Have you run away to sea
And have no time a note to pen?
So long I've searched in vain for thee!

I've climbed the mountains, slid down scree;
Tramped for miles across the fen.
Oh, my love, where can you be?
I've searched so long, in vain, for thee!

Bee Wickens

COLOURS GLOW STRONGLY WHEN THEY ARE STILL WET

Colours glow strongly when they are still wet
their luminescence adding depth to tone,
the sea's an angry azure in a fret

but, come to think of it, it's never let
to harden on a canvas or a stone,
colours glow strongly when they are still wet.

My purple ink's the best I'll ever get
for writing bawdy poems near the bone;
the sea's an angry azure in a fret

and green glass balls secure the fishing net
left floating on its gleaming depths alone -
colours glow strongly when they are still wet.

Rich jewels gain new lustre when they're set,
the sheen of gold enhancing colour tone;
the sea's an angry azure in a fret,

its white-topped riders rising higher yet
till storm winds blow the waves to crash and moan,
colours glow strongly when they are still wet,
the sea's an angry azure in a fret.

Elizabeth Bewick

TO GIVE OF PEACE
(NB a villanelle)

To give of peace, of quietness,
True Christian hearts will court despair
To search within the brokenness.

In city street, in faithfulness
Unending, love will find them there,
To give of peace, of quietness.

This love of God, which they confess,
Will take the sinner in, to care,
To search, within the brokenness.

Salvation's soldiers savour stress,
Fighting the fight, they win, who dare
To give of peace, of quietness.

And hardened heart, they love no less
(Asleep in doorway, ruined, bare,)
To search, within the brokenness.

Yet, in this shambles, in this mess,
They still find time to 'stand and stare',
To give of peace, of quietness,
To search within, the brokenness.

Roger Mosedale

MY LOVE HAS GONE

My love has gone away from me
I miss him, oh so much.
He will return, one day you will see.

I know not where he has gone
I can only wait and see
My love has gone away from me.

My love for him is so strong
I will wait forever if be
He will return, one day you will see.

Not knowing is the hardest thing.
When will my waiting be through?
My love has gone away from me.

Though his face, I cannot see
Only in my dreams.
He will return, one day you will see.

On his return, I will say I love him.
Before it's too late
My love has gone away from me
He will return, one day you will see.

Trudie Sullivan

GOODBYE TO DARTH RAMBO'S BUNGALOW

It's goodbye to the bungalow, garage and greenhouse,
And gardens, especially the one that's the rear,
All because I'm pursuing my selected future spouse.
The back garden contains a big apple tree's louse
And a pond with spawning frogs living near,
It's goodbye to the bungalow, garage and greenhouse.
It contains a frog's cage to keep grouse,
Although the frogs in their pond do appear,
All because I'm pursuing my selected future spouse.
It contains fruit bushes to feed a scouse,
Rhubarb, herbs and an underground archway sheltering fear,
Its goodbye to the bungalow, garage and greenhouse.
Tropical plants and the dummies with a blouse
Are part of interior decorating for the seer,
All because I'm pursuing my selected future spouse.
The landscape gardening will be an interior browse
And written in stories and poetry creating cheer;
It's goodbye to the bungalow, garage and greenhouse,
All because I'm pursuing my selected spouse.

Ian K A Ferguson

DID YOU KNOW?

Did you know that every single day
I am hurt and I fall down?
I just need to hide myself away.

I don't want to stay
And make you drown.
Did you know that every single day

I lay on my bed and pray
That I can laugh and be a clown?
I just need to hide myself away.

Until tomorrow becomes today
And I can throw away my frown
Did you know that every single day

I don't want to feel so grey?
To be your princess, to wear that crown.
I just need to hide myself away.

I love you in so many ways
But you need to know that I fall down.
Did you know that every single day
I just need to hide myself away?

Lindsey Brown

MONEY ISN'T EVERYTHING

Money isn't everything
This fool had lots of money
Happiness it did not bring

Once life seemed a funny thing
Now it's not so funny
Money isn't everything

I would dance, I'd laugh and sing
Life was so sunny
Happiness it did not bring

Now money has a hollow ring
It's like honey that is runny
Money isn't everything

My love she had me on a string
Called me her 'Money-bunny'
Happiness it did not bring

Now that I have flung my fling
I'm content on bread and honey
Money isn't everything
Happiness it did not bring

Norah Page

THANKS TO THE LORD

For many blessings Lord, thanks be to thee,
So many of them were made by you
And all of earth's beauties the eye can see.

The wooded glade with many a tall tree,
Marvellous scenery with mountain view,
For many blessings Lord, thanks be to thee.

Wandering through woods, happy and carefree,
the beauty of wildflower, our spirits to renew
And all earth's beauties the eye can see.

Life can be a pleasure, I'm sure you'll agree,
Communing with nature, under skies that are blue
For many blessings Lord, thanks be to thee.

How lovely on days that are free
We can walk in the country and review,
All of earth's beauties the eye can see.

As I listen to songbirds high in tree,
It is all so apparent, but very true,
For many blessings Lord, thanks be to thee.
And all of earth's beauties the eye can see.

E K Jones

THE WILY OLD FOX

I saw the hunt early yesterday morn,
it must have been out before the sun shone,
tally ho huntsman, blow your horn.

One of the riders, his red coat well worn
looking very untidy and most woebegone,
I saw the hunt early yesterday morn.

The hounds were drifting as if by scent drawn,
the fox ran ahead and was soon away gone,
tally ho huntsman, blow your horn.

The whipper-in's puzzled, his interest lukewarm,
still hoping to catch the fox thereupon,
I saw the hunt early yesterday morn.

The master is new, though not a greenhorn,
one horse has slipped on an old demijohn,
tally ho huntsman, blow your horn.

Fox slinks away, master looks drawn,
hunt returns empty, looking tired and worn
I saw the hunt early yesterday morn,
tally ho huntsman, blow your horn.

Leslie Holgate

CHILDHOOD DAYS

I miss my happy childhood days,
I wish that they could come again
I loved them in so many ways.

I loved the little Christmas plays
Which gave our mothers so much pain.
I miss my happy childhood days.

In the long summer holidays
I longed to see my friends again
I loved them in so many ways.

Birthdays at school were happy days
So many presents I would gain.
I miss my happy childhood days.

In my old age I sit and gaze
And wonder if we'll meet again
I loved them in so many ways.

When, in my rocking chair I laze
My thoughts drift to the past again.
I miss my happy childhood days
I loved them in so many ways.

Beryl Williams

ALL IS STILL

The towering hills in vibrant silence stand
The gold willows bow their heads
Dark shadows grow o'er mountain land, all is still.

Curlew calls from her meadow nest
Cool misty blanket depicts a camouflage
The towering hills in vibrant silence sand.

Sun's long fingers paint in gold
A brilliant pathway through the lea
Dark shadows grow o'er mountain land, all is still.

The towering hills in vibrant silence stand
Moon appears behind billowy clouds
Flowers bend their weary heads, pray while sheltering.

The sky's brilliant colours fade into obscurity
Stars like sapphires appear
Willows bend their golden heads

Rooks fly cawing o'er the strand
Evening's chilling fangs enfold
The towering hills in vibrant silence stand
Dark shadows grow o'er mountain land, all is still.

Frances Gibson

MY VILLANELLE

My love bought me a brass pan clock
At an auction sale one day
I turned the key it went tick tock

I hung it on the mantle top
To show the time of day
My love bought me a brass pan clock

I hoped that it would never stop
As it hung on display
I turned the key it went tick tock

York Minster graced the handle top
I polished it each day
My love bought me a brass pan clock

That unique gift kept on the dot
Time never seemed to stray
I turned the key it went tick tock

Uncertain if it would go or not
Collectable I'd say
My love bought me a brass pan clock
I turned the key it went tick tock

J Lawson

STARRY-EYED

The stars shone for you, Tony Blair,
The night you entered Downing Street,
The future seemed to be set fair.

It was a win beyond compare -
The losing Tories in retreat;
The stars shone for you, Tony Blair.

Before the dawn you would declare
New Labour's victory complete,
The future seemed to be set fair.

And good vibrations filled the air,
Born of our hopes - and I repeat
The stars shone for you, Tony Blair.

But time has passed and everywhere
The vibes move to a harsher beat;
The future seemed to be set fair.

Yet still, PM, your dreams I share;
Life for us all could be so sweet;
The stars shone for you, Tony Blair,
The future seemed to be set fair.

Sheila Burnett

DESPAIR

I remember how it rained that day
'Soaked' moaned the posing whores
In Vietnam, the end of May.

Peace ran thin, Americans would pray
Nixon you've lost, suppress your war
I remember how it rained that day.

Viet Congs, would not obey
I saw, while they mutilated more.
In Vietnam, the end of May.

Platoon in gunfire, my flashbacks play
In the depths of the jungle, the bloody core.
I remember how it rained that day.

An aftermath of silence, where families lay
Machines to thrill, there was no law.
In Vietnam, the end of May.

Taken prisoner, no tongue to say.
I wake in chains, my body raw
I remember how it rained that day.
In Vietnam, the end of May.

Jolene Neary

SUMMERTIME

Summertime with soft winds scented
  lightning strikes with wind and rain,
hungry bees on flowers rented.

Animals and birds demented
  fishermen cast lines in vain,
summertime with soft winds scented.

Cattle in fields now well contented
  whistle noise from passing train,
hungry bees on flowers rented.

Car in lane with front all dented
  sparrow hawk watches over its domain,
summertime with soft winds scented.

Flooded fields unprecedented
  water spreads over flat terrain,
hungry bees on flowers rented.

Farmers happy, now contented
  all their work was not in vain,
summertime with soft winds scented
  hungry bees on flowers rented.

Leslie Holgate

THE KILLING DOSE

Time signs the treaty for its toll,
Accursed blessing burning cold,
Scarred secret shadowed under soul.

Hope seals the pact for future holes,
Damned deity screams new to old,
Time signs the treaty for its toll.

Honesty breaks down buried gold,
Eyes run red as the tears flow,
Scarred secret shadowed under soul.

Love hides behind the heart it stole,
Joy released but for parole,
Time signs the treaty for its toll.

Hatred claims the deed its bitter own,
As pain returns for second show,
Scarred secret shadowed under soul.

End is brought to this and those,
This sacrifice the killing dose,
Time signs the treaty for its toll,
Scarred secret shadowed under soul.

Helen Marshall

FLOODING

Snow has melted, flooding holds sway,
River banks ready to explode,
The water, rollicking away,

The disaster and tragedy,
Affects the various abode,
Snow has melted, flooding holds sway.

The relentless pounding each day,
Fills the air with portent forebode,
The water, rollicking away.

Leaves nothing to imagery,
Rising, rising high on the road,
Snow has melted, flooding holds sway.

Nothing to be seen of highway,
Submerged beneath the swelling goad,
The water, rollicking away.

At last, relief may come today,
The sun is shining as does spode,
Snow has melted, flooding holds sway,
The water, rollicking away.

Mary Lawson

COME BACK TO ME

My Love, why have you left me
Feeling alone and blue?
Come back my Love, wherever you may be.

I'm looking for you, but cannot see,
You are out of view,
My Love, why have you left me?

I know that you wanted to be free,
As my love for you grew.
Come back my Love, wherever you may be.

Are you under our favourite tree?
Or, are you somewhere new?
My Love, why have you left me?

Have you gone over the sea?
Please, give me a clue.
Come back my love, wherever you may be.

I will always hope to be
The only Love you ever knew.
My Love, why have you left me?
Come back my Love, wherever you may be.

Joan Smith

ROSALIND

Perhaps you know the village quaint
Where flowers grow without restraint,
The stimulating ocean breeze,
Its cobbled streets beneath the trees.

You may hear whispers in the air
Of Rosalind, the maiden fair,
Whose singing was so clear and sweet
Along the beach and up the street.

Her tresses flowed in golden sheen,
Her eyes were of a deep sea green
And she possessed so fine a grace
That was as lovely as her face.

On stormy nights, upon the sand,
She guided fishers in to land.
To them her silver voice would sail
Across the sea upon the gale.

But then one night she disappeared
And for her safety neighbours feared.
Fair Rosalind no more was seen
Upon the beach or village green.

'Tis said that when the wind is strong
The village folk still hear her song
And fishermen throughout the bay
Still speak of Rosalind today.

Anne Greenhow

THE BALLAD OF MARY ASHFORD

Within the Midland town of Erdington, in 1817,
a curious series of events in time did unfold,
to present the world a tale never before seen,
from the distant past, this story has been told,

Mary Ashford, a twenty year old local, looking for fun,
journeyed to a local tavern, to join a special dance,
young and old were there, so many had eagerly come,
another soul there was Abraham Thornton, by chance,

Mary was so pretty and petite, with an angelic face,
here at the tavern - called the 'Three Tuns', Mary met,
Thornton, a man of bad reputation, at this place,
from then on, a sordid fate for Mary was sadly set,

Mary danced with Thornton, such a sweet naive flower,
a good time was had by all, but this joy was to end,
dancers danced and singers sang, to the early hours,
Mary was escorted outside by her new found friend,

outside, this trusting soul disappeared in the dark,
Mr Thornton arrived home safe, but alas Mary did not,
in a water pit, the dead Mary was found, so very stark,
this poor creature was violated and dumped in this spot,

the obvious was assumed, and Thornton was apprehended,
he denied any wrongdoing, but admitted intimacy with Mary,
here the true story only really begins, far from ended,
facts were few and far between, and were often contrary,

the first of two trials of Thornton began, a cause celbre,
but later on, the first trial acquitted this ogre of a man,
at the second, he used a legal ruse to save himself there,
never happening before, the law changed, so it couldn't again.

Christopher Higgins

CRUISE 2832

In 2832 I go on a cruise
Round the thirty moons of Saturn
In cabin no 510 I rest away the blues
Then I prepare to go 'ashore' on the moon Titan.

After that I venture onward
To Mimas, Iapetus, Tethy and Doone
Five days on each moon, then on forward
To Phoebe, Prometheus and Pandora alone.

Five days per satellite thirty satellites far away
Thirty times five is one hundred and fifty.
Starting Saturday 3rd June ending Saturday 27th May
One billion solar dollars to spend so thrifty.

G-ball matches, roboracing and other sport
Entertainment in big superbars
Ladies for me to make magic with of sort.
Bright lights and electricars.

End of the cruise home to Earth I go
Home to my 300 channel interactivision
Then to my cleanerobot Auntie Flow
And also to wake up from this vision!

H G Griffiths

CLADDACH MONSTER

The wailing wind and dashing sea
  Atlantic terminus
where living water meets the rock
  we're like one, you and us.

Here at Claddach Bay, power's caught
  harnessing for the grid
waves' full greeting of sea and land
  light from the light once hid.

Just standing where these forces meet
  introjecting nature
imagine a monster snoring
  fed, sleeping in capture!

The monster's snoring in the store
  is sea's power captured
God's goodness from the very deep
  use and source enraptured.

Robert D Shooter

LUCKY LIPS

Lucky lips was my heart throb
Sweeping roads was his job
He lived with his mother Gert
Who wore trousers under her skirt
Every Wednesday, Gert baked a pie
She wore a patch over one eye
Gert asked me to dinner one Sunday
I was engaged to lucky by Monday
Gert said he needed looking after
At 45, he couldn't get any dafter
So we got married on day in June
In two berth van spent our honeymoon
Lucky didn't make love, the old fashioned way
He was a funny lad, I have to say
After a while, I began to surmise
Lucky's Mum had been telling me lies
He wasn't all he was supposed to be
When I began to find out, he turned on me
He wasn't a block at all, but a wench
This discovery was a bitter wrench.
Well we talked it over, decided to try
Like two big sisters, had a good cry
Becoming companions, to each a good friend
Sharing our lives like two old hens
We've never looked back since that day
Now I'm straight and Lucky's gay.

Ann Hathaway

SPRING ON CHURCH GREEN

Before golden domes reflected,
The bright sun in the sky,
The Parish church was erected,
Crossed arrows were nearby.

The advowson we understand,
So the old book sayeth,
To Henry Earl of Cumberland,
Thirty-third of Henry the eighth.

Before the painted glass was set,
A shield stood in that place,
A lion rampant, gules de-bruised,
Near a picture of Boniface.

Close by were coaching inns and bars,
Mill chimneys in the distance,
All pointing upwards to the stars,
Like spring flowers, with insistence.

Kathleen M Scatchard

FACE TO FACE WHEN ADULT . . .

Eleven years, always in wrong
Dark eyed, muscular, hefty and strong,
Rarely at school, constant truant,
Those in charge e'er close pursuant.

He and mates considered it cool
To dictate control by gang mob rule,
Malevolence to violence
Shown, opposing his influence.

Tyranny turmoil grew apace,
Maybe soon punch sister in face,
Or cause his kin bodily harm
Non-stop aggression rang alarm.

Sent away to special needs school,
Swaggered away, inside felt a fool,
Given tests, badly colour blind,
On norm paper print lost, purblind.

Topped tinted film read masterly,
Avidly through all school library,
IQ one, three, five, a good pass,
Way above average in class.

Passed exams with flying colours
And entrance test for high school scholar,
Parents would have to support him
'Til later years knew his chance slim.

Unfortunately, they were poor
Needed him to earn money much more,
Tempted to return to old ways
But having learned, intellect stays.

Boredom reason for his conduct,
Frustrated; enraged turned to destruct,
Nowadays, owns his business,
Great compassion and tenderness.

Hilary Jill Robson

OLD PALS

Now Albert had always a musical bent
Whilst Jack was a bit of a fighter
And when Albert, playin' t'piano at t'pub,
Took th' applause for his skills
Jack just sat there and supped and got tighter

Well Albert and Jack were very good chums
They played soccer and darts and went bowlin'
And when t'war came all of a sudden like
They lost touch as t'bomb started fallin'

Now Albert he were called into t' Navy
And sailed all round t'world in a boat
Sometimes he got seasick and fell overboard
And although he couldn't swim - he could float!

Jack went into th' Army and soon got a rank
But he never got no airs and graces
His rank it were private and probably due
To his tunic wore under his braces

As a lad Bert were alus quite short for 'is height
And now as a man he seemed smaller
And Jack he were t'same alus tall for 'is height
But now as a man 'e were taller

When t'conflict were over and Hitler were beat
And twenty years more had gone by
Jack were waitin' for t'bus 'ome one Wednesday night
When Albert 'e happened to spy

Well I'll be jiggered Jack shouted to Bert
As Albert ran over to greet him
'ee 'ow you've changed said Albert to Jack
And 'ow he were so pleased to meet him

What you doin' now? said Jack - interested like
Well I'll bet you're married an' all
Aye I am answered Bert - to a nice bit o'skirt
And we've three kids - George - Ringo - and Paul!

And all of 'em interested in music like me
They play t'mouth-organ, guitar and t'drums
We'll come round to your 'ouse next Wednesday neet
We can all have a sing and be chums

Well Jack weren't best pleased though he didn't say
For wi' music he hadn't much truck
So he just bit his lip and said aye that sounds grand
We'll see thee next Wednesday with luck!

How about thee Jack? Albert enquired
Did tha' marry that big lass called Sally?
Aye I did Bert, said Jack, and we've three kids an' all
Called Patterson, Bruno and Ali

And all of 'em interested in boxing like me
And for t'punch line his tongue were abidin'
We'll come round to your 'ouse next Tuesday neet
And we'll give thee a bloody good hidin'!

Mike Dempsey

TWA LOVERS

My love and I walked down the hill
  We planned a little fun
But a stolen lorries good did spill
  And we was on the run

We laughed and laughed stopped for a while
  To see what happened next
But a fine young bobby jumped over the style
  We didn't know what to expect

Names and addresses, he took out his book
  We looked at him gone out
He cautioned us, like we was a crook
  And we began to shout

Some time later all sorted out
  We managed to make it clear
That we were lovers, just out and about
  And we all stopped for a beer!

E Corr

FATHER DIES

Father dying, pool of blood
Daughter helping? . . . if she could
Knife is ripping at his life
Far away, unloving wife!

Tries to staunch the gushing flow
Scarlet is the freezing snow
Body shivers, life ends fast
Chapter closed on painful past.

Sobbing loudly, hugs her friend
Hoped his life would never end
Kisses forehead, hands so smeared
Scene like this she always feared!

Bloody imprint in the snow
Wash away the pain and woe
With the rain, a life effaced
Down the drain his life's blood chased.

At the graveside, no more tears
Mother sighs, 'We had good years!'
Body to the ground bequeathed
For this soil of peace relieved.

David Arran

THE DEMISE OF HERMAN BRIGGS

When Herman Briggs went fishing
He had a dreadful day.
He opened up his maggots
To find flies that flew away.

He tried to bait the water
Around his chosen place,
But when he used the ground bait
The wind blew it in his face.

He sat around for hours
And didn't get a bite,
Yet full of determination,
Stayed out all day and night.

His casting was atrocious
He got tangled in the trees,
Then caught a big white swan
Who pecked him on the knees.

He caught a boot. He caught a can.
Took sunglasses from his gran,
But to his great disdain,
Roach or perch he could not gain.

Then, at last it happened,
He caught a carp upon his line.
The fish ran on, he pulled and pulled,
Thought he was doing fine.

Full of dreams of prizes,
While deciding what he'd like.
He went splash into the water,
And was eaten by a pike.

Joyce Walker

A GOOD CATCH

Then said one girl to another,
'I have got my handsome lover,
Contented I'll be ever more,
Not lonely like I was before.'

Said the second girl, 'What's his name,
You trapped him, do you feel no shame?
At him you cast your eyes of blue,
And what was the poor lad to do?'

Said girl one, 'He's glad by my side,
While I walk along filled with pride.
Says he's happy that he's found me,
He is happy as he could be.'

'You cast out your net far and wide,'
Said girl two, 'can't fault how you tried.
Bound to catch one masculine shape,
Too strong your hold, with no escape.'

'I know what our next step will be,
For he will walk up aisle with me,'
Said girl one, 'Then my task is done,
And from me then he will not run.'

S Mullinger

WICKED LORD SOULIS

A wicked Lord lived in Liddesdale,
Who dwelt in the nightmare of every child,
Whose home was desolate hermitage,
With his incubi, redcap, his trusty page,
Who rode with the devil in a rage,
Rode fast over borderland wild,
Bringing terror to the mild,
Hooves of thunder,
Mayhem and plunder,
casting the whins to turn asunder,
No one would venture out after dark,
Whilst Lord Soulis' hounds did bark,
Honest men grew sick of all this pillage,
And decided to drive him from their town and village,
No more greedy hands,
Would desecrate their farming lands,
To the castle of Hermitage they stole,
And seized Soulis, put him in a cauldron bowl,
For to damn his bloody soul,
By covering him in molten lead,
And leaving him till he was dead,
Soulis and Redcaps's screams,
Would haunt Hermitage's folks beside dreams,
And haunt it they do still,
By twilight and by whip-poor-Will,
You can hear the hounds bay o'er the hill,
Venture out if you will.

Alan Pow

THE BALLAD OF THE BROKEN-HEARTED MAIDEN

They stood on the shore in the moonlight,
Embraced and said their goodbyes.
'I'll be back in a month to wed you,
Don't fret now, dry your eyes.'

He held her close for a moment,
Then turned to the ship in the bay.
The gulls' cries sharpened her sadness
As the ship slowly sailed away.

That night the storm-clouds gathered,
And waves beat hard on the shore,
The young girl stood and waited
'Shall I ever see him a' more!'

The wind howled round about her,
The waves rushed towards her feet,
Her eyes searched the far horizon,
The rain on her face did beat.

Each day she stood and waited
Hoping to see his face.
Nothing was found but wreckage,
Of her lover there was no trace.

'Twas six long months since they parted.
She never ceased in her quest.
But they found her dead on the quay-side,
With a baby held to her breast.

Joan Thompson

SUN TODAY

When the sun appears people laugh and smile
They lay in the sun and snooze for a while
We need to make the most of the weather
It won't be long before we are clad in leather
Summertime is all too short a season
Time is against us that's the reason.

Roger Brooks

THE BALLAD OF THE BUNGAR-LILY

'Twas on a clear and shiny day
He met a lass most fair,
Bright as the merry month of May
With ribbons in her hair.

'Oh sweetest maiden marry me,'
He was heard to cry,
'Come wander o'er the grassy lea
And 'neath the moonlight lie'

'I will' said she 'if you will find
For me a bungar-lily,
For I can find no peace of mind
Though you may think me silly'

Our swain he searched by day and night
But could not find the flower,
Then thought, in any kind of light
One plant is like to t'other.

He brought her blooms so very grand
'Now marry me' he pled,
She cried 'I will not now join hand;
And tossed her pretty head.

'For bungar lilies do I yearn
Yet false you play with me,
The bungar lily, this now learn,
Is a multi-coloured tree.'

Christine Dennison

REVELATION

The girl looked up into the sky and saw thick clouds of grey,
she heard a voice quite loud and trill and here's what it did say.

'Do not marry this man' five words plain as can be,
she only had one boyfriend and thought this man it could be he.

They had not talked of marriage she thought he did not care,
he only came to see her if he could afford the fare.

But, later on they did get closer and there was a child,
the girl thought of the voice she'd heard and this made mother wild.

She said 'He is a nice boy and he's just right for you,
so, do not be so stupid and get back there in the queue.'

Now that he had won her and was liked by everyone,
he left her living with his mum they'd look but he was gone.

An argument developed, his hand went round her neck,
the mother had to stop him this made her a nervous wreck.

The next time that they argued a gun was in his hand,
she had to run off for her life the guns could have been banned.

next he would see her in her bath she liked the water high,
he thrust her under kept her down she thought her end was nigh.

If only she had listened to that voice up in the sky,
her life would have been better and might not have passed her by.

Jean Paisley

A HEART MAID OF IRON

Upon a time of trembling fools
Came madam Thatch a'spouting
A sea of bodies sunk in rage
She drowned them in her shouting

The first exception to the rule
This dame took lordly stance
She'd head a house of waltzing prinks
And lead a merry dance

Her gruesome tenure posed a boast
With selfish will displayed
Imposed a dearth throughout the land
No greater mule hath brayed

She frittered licence on the fool
To freely trade his wares
And market ostentatious trash
To rip off runtly curs

Now time has borne a greedy theme
Free enterprise for all
Where crooks and scoundrels have a share
The writing's on the wall

This British proud asylum booms
For lunatics to run
Alack! With Yankie influence
T'will soon be by the gun

While Maid Thatch rests her laurels now
With conscience unperturbed
The gates to greater lawlessness
Stay open, undisturbed

Cherry

143

THE DONKEY BALLAD

Into Jerusalem he rode
People waving palm branches
Spreading their coats for a carpet
Along the road.

Go find me a donkey
Into Jerusalem I'll ride
King on a borrowed donkey
There's a donkey at a cross-roads tied.

Jesus could have chosen a gallant steed
Rode into Jerusalem in style
He preferred he to be lowly
Never indulging in pride

King of kings on a borrowed donkey
Palm branches waving high
God's beloved Son on a borrowed donkey
Jubilation, as into Jerusalem He did ride.

Frances Gibson

LASS OR LADDIE

Come along and walk with me
Enjoy your little stroll
You'll maybe spot a rabbit
Scurrying down a hole

Some cows grazing in the fields
Sheep are in there too
No one else around - just now
Only me - and you

It's lovely just to walk in peace
No traffic whizzing past
Enjoying the beauty round about
Before it becomes o'ercast

Have you enjoyed your little stroll
In your mind's eye - with me
The countryside is beautiful
I'm sure you will agree

All of nature's little things
Birds with worm-filled beaks
In the hedgerows as you pass
You can hear the young birds squeak

Jean Logan

CORONATION. A BALLAD FOR OUR QUEEN

The Princess sat in foreign lands,
  So young and fair was she.
Her husband gently guarded her
  Who soon his queen would be.

Upon a day the message came,
  Her Father King was dead.
His daughter hid her bitter grief,
  To London turned her head.

There came the day, a happy day,
  When she received the crown.
What mattered it that now and then
  The summer rain fell down.

From end to end throughout her lands
  Hung flags from every mast.
Banners and wreaths their message gave
  That sorrow's day was past.

With music and with pageantry
  Between rejoicing crowds
Our young Queen in her coach passed by,
  Undimmed by heavy clouds.

With sacred song and solemn words
  And loud assenting cries,
Her people took her for their Queen,
  So youthful and so wise.

Her oath she swore that all her life
  She would our servant be;
God bless our Queen and give her joy
  In this new century.

Kathleen M Hatton

THE RAINBOW PEOPLE

We are they who come early or late
We are the flag-bearers of fate,
We carry a star on our brow
We are the children who plough
A furrow in the world to come,
We rattle the truth on our drum,
We pipe a song of pure joy,
The banners of love to deploy,
Heed the fantastic sweet tune,
Dance to the stars and the moon.
We're wisdom beyond all belief
We come to release you from grief,
We are your dream now come true,
The splendour that's hidden in you,
The light of the soul you forgot,
The line twixt what is and what's not.
We bring you glad tidings of hope
What's real in a world full of dope,
We sail on new oceans of light
A torch in the depth of the night,
We glide with our wings in the air,
The key to unlock your despair
We're the music of the spheres,
The smile that shines through tears -
Raise your head and gaze up high,
We're the rainbow in your sky.

Emmanuel Petrakis

147

THE UNKNOWN SOLDIER

As were those days, and the nights before,
A constant reminder, our country at war,
Death and destruction, horror and fear,
Business as usual, but shed not a tear,

As were those days, and the nights before,
The strafing, and bombing, and the killing and more,
I see my dear comrades in battle did fall,
As did many young soldiers, who answered the call,

As were those days, and the nights before,
The unknown Soldier, was called once more,
He gave not a thought, to that deadly fee,
'Twas the price of war, the fee so high,
He did answer the call, and prepared to die,

> *A hero*
> *Known*
> *Throughout this universe.*

T J Kelly

HAPPINESS

Happiness is a joy and a delight,
A mode of living when heart is light,
It's neither too low nor too high,
Has no boundaries if one will try.

Happiness a state that one can make
Much too priceless to forsake.
It belongs to the rich, and also the poor,
A blessing to the sad in search of cure.

Happiness, the cry of a new-born child,
Of a river in torrent rushing so wild;
The sun at dawn breaking through,
A yacht afloat on the ocean blue.

Happiness belongs to the young and old,
You cannot buy, yet truly hold.
Two hearts beating, true love entwine,
So odd to explain, so hard to define.

Happiness has no colour or creed,
The right of man of any breed;
It embraces all in every domain,
No one can govern, no one can reign.

Happiness was written on Calvary
Spelt in blood for you and me,
When deep in anguish and despair
Happiness you'll find in silent prayer.

William John Evans

MARINER AND THE GULLS

Where do they go, the grey gulls,
Silvery grey in the winter sky?
In twos and threes and scores they come
Mewing and laughing up on high,
The lonely sound of the lonely sea
Bringing old memories back to me.

I stand up here on this land-locked hill
Full seventy miles form the ocean's roar,
But I seem to hear, with their plaintive cries
The thunder and hiss of a sandy shore
The angry sound of the angry sea
Bringing old memories back to me.

Who can they be, the grey gulls,
Wandering, lost in the winter sky?
Ghosts of old mariners, drowned at sea,
Seeking a home that is warm and dry?
Wandering souls that are lost but free,
Bringing old memories back to me.

Soon they are gone, the grey gulls.
Whence do they come, and where do they go?
They fade from sight in the deep sea sky
Grey upon grey with flecks of snow
But tomorrow at twilight again I shall see
The grey gulls a-bringing old memories to me.

Michael Block

THE BRECON BEACONS

O Brecon Beacons bare and steep
Surrounded by so many sheep
You stand there barren, bleak and bare
In life for you there is no care
You have been there through the ages
Seen the world pass in different stages
You will still be there when I am gone
So I bid you farewell as I sing you my song
But in summer or winter in all kinds of weather
You call me to come and admire your heather
I leave my work be and rush to your side
Like a magnet you pull me, from you I can't hide
Now at last I accept and no more will fight
Because my lovelies you're a beautiful sight.

Rhiannon Jones

SECRET LOVE

Have you ever had a secret love
A love so deep inside
A love you cannot talk about
A love you have to hide?

Your every waking moment
The thoughts that are in your mind
Concealing your emotions
Of a very special kind

You try to focus on your day
Your nights are very long
This love that's out of reach for you
You wish you could belong

All you have are hopes and dreams
Of a love you cannot share
An emptiness and aching heart
And a wanting to be there

Maybe some day, in time to come
This love will come to you
So bide your time, wait patiently
For this special love so true

Maria Farrell-Grundy

THE OZONE LAYER

The ozone layer what does it do?
It keeps sun rays from me and you.
Without its shield skin cancer is rife,
And this can cause no end of strife.
So turn off the power, recycle your waste.
Give up the car, and go walking a piece.
Do all these things, and your reward will be nice,
The air will be sweet disease will be low,
And there will be happiness wherever you go.

P Davis

GRANDAD'S GARDEN

At the bottom of the garden there's hedges tall and green,
With blackberries as black and ripe as you have ever seen.
In the morning sunlight the dew upon each blade of grass,
Is like a crystal a fairy may have dropped, as she flew past.
I know it's cool there by the pond, where late summer roses bloom,
And butterflies are 'flirting' before the cold begins.
A green dragonfly settles on the hedge, a glistening magic thing.
There's runner beans and beetroot all standing in their rows,
Trees with greengages growing and apples bending low.
There's gooseberries and raspberry, a beech tree that
My brother planted . . . where we used to swing,
And a robin would be singing, waiting for grandad
to dig up the worms.
There's a pair of wellies standing by the old back door,
And onions hanging on the wall.
The old dog lies there waiting . . . looking up at me!
Yet, there is a peace in this old garden . . .
You feel it like a presence there . . .
Underneath the trees it meets you!
So that you turn and think there's someone there.
Grandad's gone to heaven . . . but,
Could he sometimes visit here?

Jennifer M Trodd

SHORTNESS OF BREATH

We had not been speaking, over some silly little thing,
So while out shopping, some flowers I thought I'd bring.
She still was not talking to me so in my chair I sat,
Because I wouldn't eat her sausages, she called me a rat.
While reading the paper, in the death column she did spy,
My name and date of birth, now she does know why.
I did not eat her sausages or answer her back,
The reason being I am dead and breathing I do lack.

Don Goodwin

THE IRISH TRIP OF DAVIE SMILLIE'S MAGIC CAR!

The time has come to tell again of Davie's magic car
Traversing on its squinty path, this time we travel far
The land upon old Erin's shore that land of green delight
The car decided it could fly, I'll tell you of its flight

Dave and cousin Ed and Davie's mate a bloke called Rob
Went across for craick and tunes, were short on a good few bob
They played a tear in one wee town, their money it was low
A local said 'You'll make some money at this Feish you know'

The Feish was held in Bally Bofey on the road went they
The three of them were high in spirits, 'twas a lovely day
Cousin Ed had fell asleep and Rab was dozing too
Davie drove without a care there was no cause for rue

The car was cunning it was smart, its mind was all its own
'I'm fed up being just a car' the engine it did moan
It had a word with all the wheels 'Let's show a bit of flare'
'To hell with all these nuts and bolts, let's fly for Ryanair'

The car decided it would fly for practice near some trees
The occupants were unaware of what was in the breeze
It left some scorch marks on the road and took off with great ease
Like the young man in the song upon the high trapeze

Consternation, constipation midst broken shards of glass
Rabe and Eddie woke with speed a tingling in their arse
A state of high awareness something said beware
The fact the car had flown, a tinge of petrol in the air

Eddie in this heightened state became a writhing snake
Houdini-like contortions with which his chains to break
The petrol fumes that teased his nostrils filled his heart with gloom
Eddie was Houdini two, freed from metal tomb

The guards arrived in Irish fashion, friendly and laid back
The questions that they asked the local centred round the craik
'Did the lads have much to drink?' They took a little drop
'In fact I'll have a pint meself, the weather's rather hot'

A music fan with big red nose, Shillelagh by his knee
Devoted to accorjun music praise for Dave had he
'Inordinately de he drink?' 'No just the right amount,
To keep his box in perfect trim past three I didn'y count'

The Guarda scratched a thoughtful chin and then says he says he
'As there was no harm done, except to that old tree
I'll write in my report book, no one had cause to cry
The car was drunk and had the notion that its wheels could fly.'

Roy Millar

HONESTLY

In my mind you're like the biggest brightest star, shining
among a million.
To my heart I declare that you don't even compare to any other.
My soul is ever willing to greet you, and feeling only a wanting
to meet you.
Like the big pure white clouds that go over in cluster, in your eyes
I could float away.
I think of you on a flowered riverside, overlooking the beauty of nature.
What you mean to me is like the gifting of life, of which you my
parents gave to me.
My hopes are that we would both be together, to love and trust one
another eternally.
If my prayers were to be answered I'd live my life with you,
within peace and in sweet harmony.
Together forever to build us a home for warm comforting security.
Always beside you, nobody can take this thought away.

Paul Smith

DIETING

I've loads of books on how to stay slim
So why am I always eating
All those lovely chocolatey things
Oh! How I love the feasting.

I know about calories and counting the fats
Eating fruit all day but I'm pining
I should be exercising or walking the dog
It always seems better reclining.

I could go to Weight Watchers
And see the pounds dropping
Would I stick to the diet?
Or eat cake when I'm shopping.

There are so many ways of losing the fat
I must turn my mind to slimming
Think of all the new clothes I could buy
If I could get down to this trimming.

I could start the diet tomorrow
Or maybe next week, I am saying
Apart from me, does anyone care?
If I'm bulky and over weighing.

I need to get me a magic pill
To take off the inches while sleeping
Until then I'll just have to stay fat
And enjoy this pleasure called eating.

Irene Cowling

ANCHOR BOOKS
SUBMISSIONS INVITED
SOMETHING FOR EVERYONE

ANCHOR BOOKS GEN - Any subject,
light-hearted clean fun, nothing unprintable
please.

THE OPPOSITE SEX - Have your say on the
opposite gender. Do they drive you mad or can
we co-exist in harmony?

THE NATURAL WORLD - Are we destroying
the world around us? What should we do to
preserve the beauty and the future of our planet -
you decide!

All poems no longer than 30 lines.
Always welcome! No fee!
Plus cash prizes to be won!

Mark your envelope (eg *The Natural World)*
And send to:
Anchor Books
Remus House, Coltsfoot Drive
Peterborough, PE2 9JX

**OVER £10,000 IN POETRY PRIZES
TO BE WON!**

Send an SAE for details on our New Year 2001
competition!